BIODEGRADABILITY AND YOU

NICHOLAS FAULKNER
AND JUDY MONROE PETERSON

rosen publishing's

rosen
central®

New York

Published in 2019 by The Rosen Publishing Group, Inc.
29 East 21st Street, New York, NY 10010

First Edition

Library of Congress Cataloging-in-Publication Data

Names: Faulkner, Nicholas, author. | Peterson, Judy Monroe, author.
Title: Biodegradability and you / Nicholas Faulkner and Judy Monroe Peterson.
Description: New York : Rosen Central, 2019 | Series: How our choices impact Earth | Audience: Grades 5–8. | Includes bibliographical references and index.
Identifiers: LCCN 2017044964| ISBN 9781508181415 (library bound) | ISBN 9781508181422 (pbk.)
Subjects: LCSH: Sustainable living—Juvenile literature. | Biodegradable products—Juvenile literature. | Recycling (Waste, etc.)—Juvenile literature. | Environmental responsibility—Juvenile literature.
Classification: LCC GE195.5 .F3725 2019 | DDC 363.7-—dc23
LC record available at https://lccn.loc.gov/2017044964

Manufactured in the United States of America

CONTENTS

All living organisms are part of Earth's life cycle. When they die, bacteria break down the remains into food that's then used by other living organisms. Those organisms, in turn, die and their remains are broken down into food for yet other organisms. And on goes the cycle. This is known as biodegrading. If Mother Nature didn't recycle, Earth would be covered with mountains of dead animals and plants from millions of years of life on Earth.

Many substances biodegrade. They're called bioactive. Bread, vegetables, and fruits break down to become simple sugars. Other materials, such as leftover hot dogs, break down into carbon, oxygen, and water. However, not all substances are biodegradable. These substances won't break down. Or they take a very long time to do so. They're considered nonbiodegradable. These substances are usually man-made chemical compounds. They include plastics, medicines, pesticides, laundry detergents, clothes, cosmetics, computers, smartphones, and more. Some plastics, for instance, can take hundreds of years to break down!

Nonbiodegradable substances do not complete Earth's life cycle and don't provide nutrients to living organisms. Bacteria that break down plant and animal waste can't recognize man-made substances. As a result, nonbiodegradable substances enter the air, water, or soil without breaking down into simpler substances. Some of these substances are harmful to the health of humans and other organisms.

Scientists develop hundreds of new chemical compounds each year and, until recently, they gave little

Plastics can take hundreds of years to biodegrade. The more plastics we manufacture, the more will accumulate in our landfills and our waterways.

thought to how these nonbiodegradable products could hurt the environment. As a result, environmental problems have been discovered after a chemical has been used for some time.

Nonbiodegradable substances are harmful to the environment in other ways, too. Companies use enormous amounts of fossil fuels to make and transport plastics and other nonbiodegradable products. The burning of fossil fuels produces greenhouse gases. These gases contribute to global warming. Global warming, which causes Earth's climate to change, is affecting ecosystems all over. If left unchecked, the production and use of nonbiodegradable substances could harm life for many years to come.

Living more sustainably, or "living green," means you're working to help the environment. This may include using biodegradable products, which will reduce your impact on the environment. People around the world are making small changes in their lives to be more planet friendly. Companies are changing their products and how they make them so they can be more environmentally safe. Governments and other organizations are setting biodegradability standards for manufacturing. Any change, small or large, will help the environment in positive ways.

By understanding which products are biodegradable and which are not, you can make better choices as a consumer. You, your family, and your friends can make planet-friendly adjustments in all aspects of your lives. Changes at home are a good way to start.

CHAPTER ONE

SHOPPING WITH MOTHER EARTH IN MIND

E very time you go to the store, you can help save the Earth. You can choose eco-friendly products. You can choose to buy organic foods, which are foods grown without chemical fertilizers or pesticides. Another way to help save Earth is to buy biodegradable clothing. While shopping, say no to plastic bags that don't biodegrade. Bring your own reusable bags, preferably made from biodegradable materials, such as organic cotton. Look for biodegradable bags made from cornstarch, vegetable oil, and other renewable resources. When eating out, try to go to restaurants that practice green policies. Support these establishments whenever possible because they are doing the same eco-friendly things that many families are doing in their homes.

GOING ORGANIC

Many of the foods in grocery stores contain added chemicals. In the United States, most grains, vegetables, and fruits are grown on huge farms called factory farms. To manage their crops efficiently, most of these farmers rely on synthetic fertilizers (plant food) and pesticides that do not biodegrade. The pesticides go into the air, water, and soil and remain on many of the vegetables, fruits, and grains that people eat. In addition, Americans eat a lot of produce (vegetables and fruits) that is grown in other countries. Much of the produce is raised on farms that use pesticides. Produce and other foods that are transported across borders generally require extra pesticides to keep from being eaten by pests.

Choosing to buy organic fruits and vegetables cuts down on the amount of chemicals in our environment that won't biodegrade.

Meat, eggs, and dairy foods such as milk come from animals that are given nonbiodegradable drugs to stop them from getting sick. Other drugs quickly increase the size of the animals. Much of the meat, dairy foods, and eggs in grocery stores and supermarkets contain these man-made drugs. Chemicals known as additives are often added to processed foods such as crackers, snacks, breads, cold cereals, and deli meats. Additives help food stay fresh longer and add color, flavor, and scent. However, additives do not biodegrade.

You and your family can buy and eat vegetables, fruits, grains, meats, eggs, and dairy foods that are organic. The U.S. Department of Agriculture (USDA) certifies that organic produce, meats, dairy products, and eggs meet specific guidelines. For example, synthetic pesticides and fertilizers cannot be used to grow certified organic foods. Check for the "USDA Organic" seal on foods. Families can buy organic foods in many grocery stores, supermarkets, health food stores, farmer's markets, food co-ops, and other stores.

Read food labels before buying. Some products may contain a mixture of organic and standard ingredients. Foods labeled "natural" may be free of synthetic chemicals. However, no national standards define what natural foods are. Natural foods are minimally processed, which means they remain as close as possible to their whole, original form. You will not find white sugar, corn syrup, white flour, margarine, and synthetic food colors or flavors in natural foods. Maple syrup and raw honey are used in natural foods instead of white sugar or corn syrup, for example.

Families can be eco-friendly by buying and eating less meat. More energy from fossil fuels is required to raise a pound of meat than a pound of grain. Farmers must grow grain to feed animals, and then the animals are processed into meat for consumers. Finally, the meat is transported to stores. All of these steps require a lot of energy from fossil fuels. It is more energy efficient for people to eat the grains, which also results in fewer greenhouse gases.

Buy local foods. Local produce requires fewer pesticides and fuel for transporting. You can find local produce at grocery stores, supermarkets, food co-ops,

Produce that's grown locally doesn't have to be shipped thousands of miles and treated with preservatives to reach your plate.

and farmer's markets. At farmer's markets, ask farmers how their produce was grown. They may grow organic vegetables and fruits, but the produce may not be certified as organic. Perhaps your family can go to local farms that sell pick-your-own berries, apples, and other produce. Some of these farms sell organic produce.

Families can join a community-supported agriculture (CSA) group. A CSA is a group of people who pledge to support a farm in return for a share of the farm's harvest. After paying a fee, CSA members receive a box of fresh vegetables and fruits from the farm every week. The produce changes with the growing season. If your family decides to join a CSA, ask if the produce is grown organically.

DRESSING ECOLOGICALLY

Clothing can be made from synthetic fibers, natural fibers, or both kinds of fibers. Synthetic fibers, such as polyester and nylon, are made by the chemical processing of oil (petroleum). Natural fibers come from silk, cotton, bamboo, trees, corn, and other plants. Sheep, alpaca, and other animals provide natural fibers. Prized for their fiber, alpacas are herd animals that are originally from South America.

The threads and fabrics used to make clothing go through many processing steps, including spinning, dyeing, weaving, cleaning, and sizing. Huge amounts of energy, water, and chemicals are required to process, produce, package, and transport clothes made from synthetic fibers or natural fibers.

You may think that using natural fibers in clothing would be a good way to be eco-friendly. However, farmers use large amounts of synthetic pesticides to grow cotton and produce wool. Chemicals like dyes and bleaches are often added to cotton and wool during the processing steps. Clothes that are labeled as permanent press, easy care, no wrinkle, no ironing, or crease resistant have chemical finishes. The synthetic chemicals that are used to make clothes with natural fabrics are nonbiodegradable.

Sometimes, clothes labeled "natural" include fabrics made from rayon, lyocell, or acetate. The term "natural"

Many fabrics are manufactured with materials that are not necessarily eco-friendly or biodegradable. Check to see what your clothing is made from.

has no national standards, which means the clothing may not be eco-friendly. Rayon, lyocell, and acetate are made from cellulose, a plant fiber that comes from trees. The processing of cellulose into threads and fabrics requires many chemicals, and most of the cellulose from the trees is thrown away during processing.

To be eco-friendly, you and your family can buy clothes made from plants or wools that are sustainable, organic, and will readily biodegrade. Check for labels that list organic cotton, organic wool, bamboo, hemp, or linen—a fabric made from the flax plant. In addition, check the label for organic certification by a state agency or an organization independent of the maker of the fabric. Organic cotton is used for many kinds of everyday, work, and sports clothes. Bamboo, hemp, and linen are hardy plants, grow quickly, and don't require pesticides.

Most dyes for clothes are made from oil. Look for low-impact colorings when buying clothes, or buy organic clothing that is not dyed. Cotton grows in shades of natural, blue, green, brown, and purple. Minerals and irons found in the earth are used to dye fabrics red, yellow, orange, and other colors. Fiber from sheep and alpaca come in more than a dozen natural colors and can be blended to produce other colors. You can find earth-friendly clothes at malls, local stores, or on the internet. Some clothing store chains sell organic clothes and underwear. For rainy weather, people can buy umbrellas made from renewable bamboo, which biodegrades in one to two years.

You can find some cool clothes at thrift and vintage shops. Not only do you get trendy, high-quality attire, you also are able to salvage what might have gone into a landfill.

Another way to go green is to buy fewer clothes. Then, less energy is used to produce and transport clothing, which reduces the amount of nonbiodegradable products and greenhouse gases that go into the environment. You can also buy used clothes at secondhand or thrift shops, yard sales, or on the internet. Try swapping clothes with family members and friends. You will be helping the Earth—and saving money!

KNOW WHAT TO EAT

Many people eat in restaurants or buy food and beverages that they consume in the car, at sports events, at work, and so on. Students can buy meals, snacks, and beverages at school. Vending machines at malls, schools, and other places stock soda, juice, water, chips, and candy. Making some small changes can help make eating out more eco-friendly.

You can choose to eat at restaurants offering organic, natural, and local foods. Some restaurant owners and chefs grow and use their own organic vegetables and herbs. Find out if biodegradable utensils,

WHAT'S ON YOUR SHOPPING LIST?

Today, companies are realizing that consumers want to be planet friendly, so they're making more green products than ever.

For your home, some of the biodegradable items you can buy are trash bags, dish soap, paper towels, toilet paper, diapers, fertilizers, and more. For school and work, you can purchase biodegradable printer paper, folders, cardboard boxes, pens, and rulers, to name just a few.

Try to buy eco-friendly products that don't have synthetic chemicals, including fragrances, preservatives, colors, and detergents. Instead, choose all organic ingredients. If you can't find organic products, carefully read the list of ingredients. The shorter the list of ingredients, the better the product is, especially if the product contains natural and herb extracts, minerals, and oils.

dishes, cups, and takeout containers like bowls, cups, and boxes are used. Biodegradable straws made from paper are available. Be sure that chopsticks are made from a sustainable plant like bamboo. Use containers that restaurants provide to recycle biodegradable tableware and food scraps. You can also ask if the containers are made from biodegradable plants, such as corn, and if the restaurant disposes of food scraps by composting.

People can encourage restaurants to provide tableware and takeout containers that are environmentally friendly. Some cities have passed laws about the use of takeout containers that are nonbiodegradable. According to the organization Earth911, more than one hundred cities have banned restaurants and supermarkets from using takeout cups, containers, and other dishes made of polystyrene foam. Often called foam, this plastic is formed into small beads, which are then made into a variety of disposable (throwaway) containers. Most cities banning foam takeout containers require biodegradable containers for food and beverages.

Visit local eateries. Eating locally reduces the production of nonbiodegradable substances and greenhouse gases by decreasing the energy needed for transportation. Local restaurants can offer a variety of interesting and tasty foods. In addition, local businesses help create jobs, which helps the community.

CHAPTER TWO

WATCHING YOUR WASTE

There are two main types of waste that come out of households: solid waste and wastewater. Trash is a solid waste. Garbage ranges from packaging, food scraps, and grass clippings to old computers, sofas, and clothes. Packaging includes plastic wrap, milk cartons, cereal boxes, and cardboard. Wastewater, also called gray water or sewage, is water from the tap, toilet, shower, tub, and washing machine.

Most trash and food waste from households goes into landfills, which are large holes in the ground. Each hole has a thick, plastic liner between the ground and the trash. After waste is dumped into a landfill, it is compacted (crushed). A layer of soil is added to cover the trash, and then the waste is compacted again. Over time, a landfill forms into a large hill with layers of waste and soil. Landfills are carefully designed to prevent waste from mixing with soil and water in the ground and to reduce odors as the waste decomposes (breaks down). Some of the waste in landfills slowly decomposes, forming greenhouse gases that go into the atmosphere. Substances that are not biodegradable can leak into the water and soil.

We don't realize that when we throw away those disposable utensils or old electronics, they pile up in heaping landfills and will take countless years to break down.

Since 1960, the amount of solid waste generated by Americans has steadily increased. Although the population has also grown during this time to about 323 million in 2016, the amount of solid waste produced per person has increased. In 2014, according to the Environmental Protection Agency (EPA), paper and cardboard made up about 27 percent of the solid waste in the United States. Other solid waste categories were yard waste at 13 percent, food waste at 14 percent, and plastics, also at 13 percent. Metals were the next largest group, followed by wood, glass, and other wastes. In 2014, the EPA estimated that Americans generated about 258 million tons (234 million metric tons) of trash.

Most materials that make up solid waste are either biodegradable or recyclable. However, most plastics don't biodegrade. In addition, plastics are more difficult to recycle than paper, yard, food, glass, wood, clothes, leather, and other wastes. One problem is that many kinds of plastic exist. Another problem is that different plastics remelt at different temperatures. Remelting is the first step in recycling processes.

REDUCE, REUSE, RECYCLE

Most goods that families buy and bring home end up as garbage sooner or later. Materials and energy are needed to make, transport, and get rid of belongings that people no longer want. Trash contains substances that don't biodegrade—or could biodegrade if they were composted. To reduce the amount of trash dumped into landfills, you and your family can follow the 3 R's: reduce, reuse, and recycle. To "reduce" means to use less of something. Reducing leaves less trash that can be thrown away, reused, or recycled. To "reuse" means to use something again, and to "recycle" means to prepare waste for reuse.

Reducing is more important waste management than reusing or recycling. Buying less saves natural resources and reduces the amount of nonbiodegradable substances that are used to make and transport things. For example, try not to buy disposable, or throwaway, products. Encourage your family to use products that last, for example, using china instead of paper plates. Instead of paper towels, clean up spills with washable cloths.

Families can reuse and repair objects and equipment around the home. Clean, empty egg cartons, plastic containers, and glass jars can be reused as storage containers, for example. You can reuse scrap paper before recycling it. Your family might repair tools, machines, and appliances instead of buying new products. For instance, metal tools with screws generally can be fixed. Quality clothes made from organic fabrics typically last a long time and don't come apart when washed. A number of good books and websites provide ideas for reusing everyday things and explain how to make household repairs.

SO MUCH PACKAGING

Packaging is anything wrapped around or attached to a product. The main packaging materials are paper, cardboard, glass, aluminum, steel, wood, and plastics. Making and transporting packaging uses enormous amounts of fossil fuels and water, and it produces a variety of nonbiodegradable materials.

Some packaging is useful. It protects foods, such as peanut butter or jam, from damage and spoiling during shipment, and it helps make products easier to handle. Packaging can provide important information. You and

With the rise of online shopping, we're producing more packaging than ever in the form of cardboard shipping boxes and other types of packaging.

your family read labels to learn how to prepare food or find the correct dosage of a medicine. Many products, though, come with a lot of packaging. For example, new televisions are often packed in boxes, plastic bags, and plastic foam. Looked at a boxed, frozen meal and note that it has a paper box, a foil or plastic tray that holds the meal, and plastic wrap that covers the food. Families can buy products with less packaging. They can buy foods like cereals in large, rather than single-serving, containers. By going to the bulk food sections of stores, consumers can put only the amounts that they want into containers. Cookies, chips, and other foods come in biodegradable bags that can be composted later.

Look for detergents and cleaners in ultra or concentrated forms because these containers are smaller than the regular products. Use bar soaps instead of liquid wash to save packaging. Cut back on wrapping waste by putting gifts in reusable bags or baskets. Tie gifts with biodegradable ribbons of raffia, a natural fiber. Some shipping stores will accept foam packing peanuts from households to reuse when sending packages.

RECYCLING REVOLUTION

The amount of energy needed to change recyclable materials into new products is often smaller than that required to generate new materials. However, energy is still required to transport, sort, and process recycled materials to make new products. Nonbiodegradable chemicals are still used and produced during the recycling process. Recycling, though, is a good and important idea. Many communities provide recycling programs. People sort their recyclable waste into different groups: glass, metals (aluminum and steel), most paper, and plastics. Trucks pick up the sorted recyclables from households along street curbs, or

Many towns and cities have mandatory recycling programs. Look into the rules and recycling pickup days in your own community.

people bring their recyclables to a central site (drop-off center).

Some recycling programs accept most plastics, while other programs take only certain kinds of plastics. Different kinds of plastics require different recycling processes. The plastics identification code of numbers 1 to 7 reveals the kinds of plastic. The codes are usually stamped on the bottom of containers.

Number 7 plastics include bioplastics, which are plastics made from biodegradable plants. Corn is the most commonly used plant in biomaterials that are made into plastic. Some disposable tableware comes from potatoes. You and your family can buy an ever-growing number of products made from bioplastics, including gift cards, clothes, water bottles, and food containers. Scientists are developing new bioplastics from vegetable oils, sugar cane, sugar beets, wheat, rice, soybeans, sweet potatoes, switch-grasses (grasses that are used to feed farm animals), and cassavas (roots that are eaten).

Most bioplastics can't be tossed into compost piles at home. Bioplastics require the high temperatures that a large, industrial compost site provides. Some companies are working to make bioplastics that can be composted at home, right along with food or yard waste. Other companies are developing bioplastics that will decompose at sea in the salty water.

Products made from bioplastics assure a decreased need for fossil fuels, but they are not the total answer to slow the growth of global warming. As bioplastics are made, carbon dioxide is released into the air, which contributes to global warming. The crops needed to make biomaterials require land and water to grow. In addition, recycling biomaterials can be a problem. Plastics with recycling codes 1 through 6 can be recycled into other products. Code 7 products include bioplastics and all other plastics that don't fit into codes 1 to 6. Most recycling sites send code 7 plastics to landfills. The plastics industry developed the seven codes for plastics. In time, perhaps another code num-

A "NEAT" IDEA

Scientists have estimated there are five trillion pieces of plastic in the world's oceans. In the North Pacific Ocean, there's one region where the ocean garbage has collected and formed a virtual trash island. Called the Great Pacific Garbage Patch, it spans from the West Coast of North America to Japan. Scientists think there are probably hundreds of thousands of tons of garbage in the patch.

One young person is looking to clean it up. Boyan Slat was just seventeen when he announced his idea in 2011. Started in 2018, he plans to clean up tens of thousands of tons of ocean trash a year using a device that floats in the ocean and acts as an "artificial coastline," which catches debris and collects it in a central location. It will then be gathered and recycled. He expects to collect 50 percent of the total trash in just five years!

ber will be created for bioplastics as their use continues to grow and methods to compost them increase.

Most food wastes go into the trash and finally are dumped into landfills. However, food scraps are biodegradable. Food scraps and other biodegradable items often take a long time to biodegrade in landfills. This is because landfills are compacted tightly and lack the oxygen needed to break down molecules quickly. The degrading process for biodegradable materials can be sped up by composting, or recycling, in the home in compost containers or in outside compost piles. Perhaps you and your family already put grass clippings, leaves, and dead plants in a compost pile.

Finished compost that is added to yard and garden soil provides many nutrients. Compost made from food and yard waste saves money that your family might otherwise spend on fertilizer for the yard and garden. Your family will also save money by not needing to buy plastic bags for trash and yard waste.

Composting can occur quickly. Bread breaks down in a few days. Paper biodegrades in two to five weeks, and a cardboard milk carton takes five years to compost.

WHERE DOES YOUR WATER GO?

Wastewater is all the water that has been used by you and your family and that goes down the drain in your home. Wastewater comes from the kitchen sink, toilet, showers, baths, and washing machines. Governments and water supply agencies recycle wastewater in sewage (waste) treatment plants and then mix the water with fresh water drawn from rivers or lakes. This high-quality water is what you drink and use in your home. Solid waste that is separated from wastewater is often dumped into landfills.

Some wastewater, called gray water, can be reused. Water from washing machines, kitchen sinks, showers, and baths usually contain only small amounts of nonbiodegradable substances. Families can use gray water on their lawns and gardens. Avoid reusing blackwater, which is water from toilets.

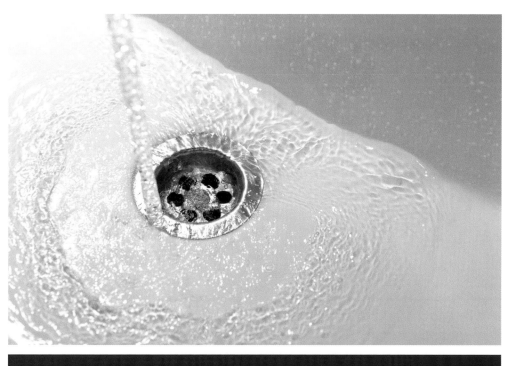

Water that goes down shower and sink drains is called gray water. Though obviously not drinkable, it can still be used for things such as watering the garden.

You and your family can take steps to be more eco-friendly with water. One step is to compost food scraps instead of running them through the garbage disposal in the kitchen sink. Garbage disposals use energy and water to run. The ground-up food in the wastewater loads sewage treatment plants with food waste that is biodegradable. Another step is to put tap water into reusable bottles or other containers instead of buying bottled water. Plastic bottles of water are costly to produce and transport, and they use huge amounts of resources and energy from fossil fuels. Currently, only a few companies worldwide are making biodegradable plastic bottles for water. Recycle plastic water bottles.

Remember to take unwanted medicines out of their original containers and throw them in the trash. You can also take medicines to a pharmacy for safe disposal. Never flush unwanted medicines down the toilet or put them down the drain. Many medicines don't biodegrade and pass through sewage treatment plants and septic systems untreated. As a result, very small amounts of different kinds of drugs are in the recycled water that communities use. Scientists don't yet know the effects of these drugs on people and animals that live in water, such as fish.

CHAPTER THREE

CARING FOR EARTH STARTS AT HOME

A re you feeling helpless in the fight to save Mother Earth? Well don't. There's a lot you can do, starting at home. Make sure you read labels and only buy eco-friendly products for the home. Look for any ingredient ending in "-ene" or "-ol," or with "phenol" or "glycol" in its name. Avoid using these products because they contain one or more nonbiodegradable ingredients. Using eco-friendly products in and around your home also can be good for your health. Regular paints, cleaners, glues, and finishes can release small amounts of poisons throughout your home. These poisons can be harmful to your family's health and the health of your pets.

CLEAN GREEN

Many cleaners sold in stores leave kitchens, bathrooms, and other rooms sparkling with a "clean" odor. Some people use an all-purpose, or general purpose, cleaner. Others prefer different cleaners for specific chores in the home. Families might stock a cabinet or shelf with cleaners for dishes, countertops, stoves, sinks, or ovens. They might tackle tubs, showers, windows, mirrors, furniture, carpets, or floors with other cleaning products. To clean and produce a gloss on metal pots and pans, some people apply polishes.

The sparkle, gloss, and smell of these cleaners come from the nonbiodegradable substances in them. These substances are synthetic chemicals made from fossil fuels that damage the environment. For example, cleaning products in spray cans release greenhouse gases into the home, which then move into the atmo-

There are countless cleaning products on the market, and they often accumulate under the kitchen sink or in the closet. Many of these products are not as green as you might think.

sphere. You breathe in the greenhouse gases and absorb them through the skin. In addition, many cleaners that are made from some fossil fuels irritate or burn people's skin and are poisonous if swallowed.

The Environmental Protection Agency (EPA) regulates chemicals that might be a risk to the environment. The Consumer Product Safety Commission (CSPSC) oversees the safety of household cleaning products. These agencies, however, have not determined the risk or safety of most cleaners. By law, chemical companies must put storage and first-aid information on the labels of their products. The law does not require them to list the chemicals and other substances in their products. Sometimes, companies put "color" or "fragrance"—or other terms like "fresh scent," "mountain scent," or "clean smelling"—on their product labels. They never explain that these are terms for nonbiodegradable chemicals.

As a first step, you and your family can reduce your use of nonbiodegradable cleaners. Check the labels of cleaners for words like "Danger," "Poison," "Warning," or "Caution." These signal words alert people that the chemicals in the cleaners often don't biodegrade and are poisonous to living organisms. Instead, use cleaners that are labeled biodegradable and don't have synthetic fragrances or dyes. Biodegradable cleaners are made from plant-based oils and natural minerals, such as calcite and feldspar. Say no to air fresheners and sprays— open windows to let in fresh air. Flowers, sweetgrass, pinecones, or conifer branches bring natural plant odors indoors. Later, the plants can be composted.

Before synthetic products became available, people used natural cleaners. Homemade cleaners readily biodegrade, are easy to make, and save money. You and your family can make cleaners with earth-friendly ingredients, including vinegar, baking soda, hydrogen peroxide, plant-based oils, and castile soap or another vegetable-based soap. A number of books and websites discuss how to make natural cleaners for the home. Remember to use biodegradable scrubbers like natural sea sponges and loofahs, a gourdlike plant. If you use cellulose sponges, be sure they are biodegradable and made of wood from renewable tree farms.

ECO-FRIENDLY LAUNDRY

When washing clothes, bed linens, towels, and other laundry, many families use stain removers and detergents made from fossil fuels to clean and add fragrance. Dryer liquids and sheets coat laundry with fragrances and other chemicals that make the family wash feel soft and free of wrinkles. Like many household cleaners, most stain removers, detergents, and dryer liquids and sheets contain large numbers of nonbiodegradable chemicals.

Eco-friendly laundry detergents and fabric softeners are made from plants or natural minerals that readily biodegrade, such as plant seeds, citrus fruits, vegetable oils, and other natural oils. You can make your own stain remover by mixing baking soda or cornstarch with cold water to form a paste. Gently rub the paste on the stain, and then pop the clothing into the laundry. Hydrogen peroxide, available at many stores, can remove stains, too.

You might already have all the ingredients you need to make your own laundry detergent. Not only will you have a green product, you'll also save money.

You and your family can make laundry soap by using biodegradable liquid soap or detergent, baking or washing soda, and vinegar. To whiten clothes, tablecloths, and other things, add natural ingredients like lemon juice, oxygen bleach, or a mix of washing soda and hydrogen peroxide to the wash. Look for laundry cleaner recipes that use natural ingredients. Another natural cleaner for laundry is soap nuts, the dried fruit of the soapberry tree. The soaplike substance in the fruit works like laundry soap.

RESPONSIBLE LAWN AND GARDEN CARE

Some families enjoy having a green lawn. They might also care for flowers, shrubs, and trees in their yards. To get lush growth, some people put synthetic pesticides and fertilizers on or near their green living plants. Others hire lawn services that spray an array of chemicals on the grass. In both cases, many of the products used to treat pests and fertilize plants contain chemicals that are nonbiodegradable.

Chemical lawn services may put up warning signs on lawns after spraying to warn people that the lawn has been

THE EARTH-FRIENDLY BEDROOM

Besides sleeping, many teens spend a lot of time in their bedrooms doing schoolwork, talking to friends, listening to music, and playing video games. Making some changes can result in more eco-friendly bedrooms. If your family is making some changes in your home, perhaps your family can use biodegradable wool carpeting or flooring from sustainable wood or bamboo. Plants that are sustainable grow very quickly and require much less energy from fossil fuels to harvest and produce things that people need or want.

Look at your mattress. Companies often treat mattresses with chemicals made from fossil fuels to retard (slow down) fire and resist water, stains, and wrinkles. Untreated, organic cotton or wool mattresses that biodegrade are better for the environment—and for sleepers.

Use organic cotton, organic wool, hemp, organic bamboo, or wild silk sheets, pillowcases, mattress pads, and comforters instead of standard bedding that is treated with fabric finishes. These chemical finishes help repel stains and wrinkles but are not biodegradable. Sleep on pillows made from organic cotton, organic wool, organic bamboo, or kapok, which are the seedpods from kapok trees. Be sure to use kapok from sustainable trees.

To store bedding, clothes, books, and other items, use furniture and containers made from plants that are sustainable. A variety of plants are made into chairs, tables, baskets, ottomans with storage space, and chests. Some of these plants include abaca (also called bacbac), rush, seagrass, vetiver root, rattan, and bamboo. See if the furniture was made with eco-friendly glues or finishes.

It might be time for a fresh coat of paint on your bedroom walls. An open can of paint or a newly painted bedroom has a certain odor. That smell comes from the many synthetic chemicals that are in standard paints. To lessen the impact to the environment, use paints that are water based instead of oil based. You can also use eco-paints.

The next time you want to change the color of your bedroom, choose an eco-friendly paint. There are more and more on the market every day.

In contrast to standard paints, eco-paints don't contain synthetic plastics and other nonbiodegradable chemicals. Instead, they are made of biodegradable substances, such as linseed oil, citrus oils, tree resins, waxes, and china clay (clay that occurs naturally), making them better products for the environment.

Insulation in the walls and around windows in bedrooms and other rooms helps keep heat indoors during cold months. If your family is adding insulation, ask if it can be biodegradable. One kind of biodegradable insulation is made from mushrooms spores. Wool fiber and hemp are other types of biodegradable insulation.

treated. However, dogs and cats track the chemicals inside the house. Children who can't read yet might

The chemicals we spray on our lawns may make the grass look pretty, but they're often made from harsh ingredients that will stay around for many years.

play on the treated lawn, absorbing chemicals through their skin and bringing them into the house on their footwear. Nonbiodegradable chemicals that kill pests also affect wild animals and beneficial insects.

Ask your family to find out what products the lawn service company sprays with and how often they service lawns. If the pesticides and fertilizers are nonbiodegradable, have your parents ask if the service can change to natural products. Or switch to a natural lawn care service, if available. Consider planting native plants and natural grasses that require fewer, if any, pesticides and fertilizers than standard lawn grasses. Some families have replaced their standard grass lawn with an eco-lawn mix of natural grasses, clovers, wildflowers, and herbs. Eco-lawns need less spraying and fertilizing than standard lawn grasses. As a bonus, these lawns don't require much water or mowing, which saves natural resources.

A growing number of families are raising their own vegetables and fruits. You and your family can try organic gardening by using natural products to feed plants and control pests. However, avoid gardening products that are made from fossil fuels. You can use biodegradable garden pots made from bamboo, paper, rice, corn, wheat, or peat.

MYTHS & FACTS

Myth: Most of the biodegradable waste generated in the United States is composted.
Fact: In the United States, the great majority of solid waste goes to landfills. Some is burned in incinerators, or large furnaces. Only a small percentage of solid waste is composted or recycled.

Myth: Because the ocean is vast, it can absorb the trash that people throw into it. Trash sinks to the bottom of the ocean and does not create problems for the environment.
Fact: The ocean currents bring trash together in concentrated areas. This action creates large floating islands of trash, especially plastic trash, that will not biodegrade for hundreds of years. Floating trash islands in the sea are constantly growing.

Myth: It is a good idea to burn trash that cannot biodegrade.
Fact: Burning nonbiodegradable trash, such as plastics, releases poisonous chemicals into the air. Some poisons attach to raindrops, which then spread across the earth. When the rain falls from the sky, the poisons go into the groundwater and soil. Other poisons are left in the ashes, which are sometimes dumped on the ground or into water.

CHAPTER FOUR

SUSTAINABLE COMMUNITIES

We all are part of larger networks, whether it's your family, your town, or your country. The eco-friendly habits that you form can spread throughout your community much faster than you think.

If you camp in local, state, or national parks, use washing and cleaning products that are biodegradable. Use biodegradable bags to collect and recycle waste. When fishing in lakes or rivers, use biodegradable bait instead of plastic bait. When fish eat plastic, they cannot digest it or bring it back up from their stomachs and out their mouths. The plastic stays in their stomachs, and the fish may die if they eat too much of it.

You can take other green steps. Be part of community, business, or other programs that safely dispose of products containing nonbiodegradable materials. Learn about the eco-labeling of products and how you might invest in living green. You can write letters to the editors of local newspapers and decision makers about biodegradable issues and solutions.

RALLY TOGETHER

Many communities offer green programs for their residents. Take part in eco-programs that are offered in your area.

Every year in the United States, pet dogs produce millions of pounds of waste. Most dog waste goes to landfills. Some businesses provide a new service to dog owners. People get biodegradable bags from these companies. When the bags are full, the owners return them, and the businesses compost the bags and waste or send everything to sites that can do the composting.

You and your pet can be eco-friendly together with biodegradable bags. What might seem like waste can actually be reused.

Remember that dog or cat waste should not go into home compost piles because they don't get hot enough to kill microorganisms that could cause diseases.

The county solid waste center may provide a central compost site. Some centers also have compost drop-off sites throughout a city or an area. Families can bring yard waste in biodegradable bags to these sites. A growing number of communities have industrial compost sites. Bacteria are used to quickly biodegrade plant, meat, and dairy waste. Food scraps come from grocery stores, nursing homes, hospitals, colleges, and other organizations in the community. In turn, the sites sell the rich compost to the community.

Communities may have hazardous waste and drug take-back programs. Hazardous, or harmful, material is in some household products like antifreeze, batteries, paint, fluorescent bulbs and tubes, and more. Improper disposal of these products can harm groundwater, cause fires, and injure people and animals. Through a community program, residents can bring hazardous materials to a central site for safe disposal. In drug take-back programs, residents can give unwanted medicine to local pharmacies or a central location in the community for proper disposal.

MIGHTY MICROORGANISMS

Bioremediation is the process of using bacteria and other microorganisms to treat chemical leaks or spills on soil or in groundwater. Bacteria and other microorganisms constantly break down dead plants and animals in soil and water. If oil or other chemicals spill into an area, some natural microorganisms would die. Others would live and eat the chemical. Bioremediation provides fertilizer, oxygen, and other substances to the chemical-eating organisms. The added materials cause the microorganisms to grow rapidly, and, in turn, the microorganisms break down the spilled chemical quickly.

Bioremediation is often used to clean up oil spills on land or water. However, bioremediation may not work on chemicals that are poisonous to most micro-organisms. Some metals and salts, such as sodium chloride (table salt), kill most bacteria. Bioremediation works on oil and other chemicals at the location where they were spilled. Large amounts of soil or water don't need to be dug up or pumped out of the ground to be treated.

To decrease the risk of future spills, all families should use less oil, electricity, and gas, too, which are made from oil. If less oil is required in the United States, not as much oil needs to be transported. You and your family can help by buying fewer products that are not needed. Walk, ride a bicycle, or take the bus instead of traveling by car whenever possible. Have your family bring oil or oily waste to a hazardous waste site for disposal instead of dumping it in the garbage or sewer. If an oil spill occurs in your area, ask if you can help in the cleanup work.

BIOREMEDIATION IN PRACTICE

In December 2016, the nonprofit organization INTACH (The Indian National Trust for Art and Cultural Heritage) attempted to clean up the highly polluted Assi river in Varanasi, India, using bioremediation. The river runs through highly populated areas where waste is dumped directly into the flowing waters. Floating garbage made treatment difficult. The bacteria, designed to break down pollutants, enhance oxygen levels, and remove odors, was added to the water every day at six locations.

Within one month, residents near the river reported that the smell had reduced. Water tests also showed great improvement. Pictures of a glass of river water also showed a dramatic change. Before, the water was brown and cloudy. Afterward, it was almost perfectly clear.

ECO-INVESTING

Investing in stocks, bonds, or mutual funds is an opportunity to earn more money than you might in a savings account in a bank. Some people are investing in Earth-friendly companies. You can invest in stocks, bonds, or mutual funds at any age, but your parent or guardian is the owner of your investment until you become eighteen years old.

Eco-companies might be involved in developing bioplastics or renewable energy, growing organic foods, or using sustainable plants to make clothes. Some green companies use biodegradable packing peanuts, inks, and cleaning products.

One way to invest is to buy the stocks of a green company. Stocks are an investment in the ownership of a business. If the value of the stock goes up, the company pays you money when you sell the stock. A company might also pay you dividends, which are the part of the company's profit that it pays to its stockholders. If the

Wall Street will recognize the power behind biodegradable products when people start investing in the companies that make those products.

company does poorly, families might lose some or all of their investments.

Eco-friendly mutual funds are another option for investing. A mutual fund is a pool of money run by trained professionals. The professionals invest in a mix of stocks and other investments. Every mutual fund has a different level of risk and opportunities to earn money.

A great way to learn about investing is to join investment clubs, which are offered in many high schools and colleges. A teacher supervises as students invest real or virtual (make-believe) money. Parents or guardians must sign a partnership agreement so that students under the age of eighteen can invest real money. An adult also must place the orders to buy and sell stocks. Whether using real or virtual money, students research companies, decide what stocks to buy, and track their stocks' performance.

"DIRTY" TRICKS

Buying and using Earth-friendly products is one way to make a difference for the earth. However, some companies claim to follow green practices but really don't. "Greenwashing" is the practice of making a company or its products appear to be eco-friendly. Before buying from a company, determine if its products, services, and way of doing business are really green. Read labels and study any green claims.

Some companies put words such as "biodegradable," "eco," "natural," "environmentally friendly," "eco-friendly," or "nontoxic" (not poisonous) on their labels and packaging. Federal and state governments don't regulate the use of these words, and usually the words don't mean anything. The word "recyclable" on a label or package means only that you can recycle a product or packaging. The word "recycled" indicates that a company used recycled materials to make the product or package.

Some companies use packaging with soft, clean colors for a natural look. However, pink roses on a jug of laundry cleaner may not mean the soap is made from flowers. Read the ingredient label. You may discover that the laundry soap has man-made fragrance so that it smells like roses. Be sure that you and your family look carefully at the labels of bio-based plastics. Some are made from biodegradable plants. Others come from a mix of petroleum and materials from plants, and these products don't biodegrade.

Look at product labels to find information about the green claims made by a company. If this information is not on the label, see if the company's website or phone number is listed. The company's website may have more information about its products. If you have any questions about green claims, call or e-mail the company. If you can't find any way to contact the company, the product may not be eco-friendly.

Check for certification by trustworthy organizations on products or their packaging. Foods meeting the U.S. Department of Agriculture (USDA) standards for organic content can display the "USDA Organic" seal. Another federal program, called Energy Star, helps protect the environment by certifying those products that use energy efficiently. Some products in this program include battery chargers, TVs, computers, laptops, printers, and more. Products that meet the standards carry the Energy Star logo.

The Canadian government started the EcoLogo program in 1988. Today, EcoLogo certifies products worldwide. Products that meet its strict standards display the EcoLogo logo. Green Seal is the largest eco-labeling organization in the United States and certifies many kinds of con-sumer products. A product must meet strict environ-mental standards to carry the Green Seal label. Look for the Forest Stewardship Council (FSC) logo on wood and paper products to certify that the wood came from well-managed forests. Products with the FSC logo are available worldwide.

TAKE CHARGE!

It's important to make changes in your own life.

You can help other people and organizations make eco-friendly choices by sharing your knowledge about green matters and biodegradability. You can express your opinions about biodegradability issues, influence other people, and help create change.

Start by writing an article for your school newspaper, or write a letter to your local newspaper or state rep-

Teaming up with others is the best way to spread the word about the importance of choosing biodegradable products and eco-friendly lifestyles.

resentatives. Describe a biodegradability issue and a solution. For example, you might ask that local schools serve lunch using biodegradable dishes, forks, knives, and spoons. Organize students to encourage local schools to send their biodegradable waste to an industrial compost site, start their own compost pile, create organic gardens for students, and buy foods for school lunches from local farms.

Man-made products that don't biodegrade have a direct effect on the environment. All the nonbiodegradable substances that people have ever made, used, and thrown away are still on Earth. By making small changes, you can reduce your use of nonbiodegradable substances. All changes, small and large, will add up to some very big changes that will help planet Earth and all of the living beings on it.

TEN GREAT QUESTIONS
TO ASK YOUR SCIENCE TEACHER

1. What elements biodegrade?
2. What organisms help things biodegrade?
3. What environmental conditions determine how long materials take to biodegrade?
4. Will a glass jar biodegrade?
5. How long does it take for common objects to biodegrade, such as a potato, orange peels, a tin can, and a pair of cotton jeans?
6. What biodegrades the fastest: a dead oak tree, a wood pencil, or a small wood box?
7. Why do closed composters biodegrade materials faster than open compost piles?
8. What are some possible environmental problems with biodegradable plastics?
9. If an astronaut drops an apple on the surface of the moon, will it biodegrade?
10. Are the fossil bones of dinosaurs biodegradable?

GLOSSARY

additive A chemical that helps foods stay fresh longer and might also add color, flavor, and scent.

biodegradability The ability of substances to be broken down into simpler substances by bacteria.

biodegrade To break down substances into simpler substances by bacteria.

bioplastics Plastics that are made from plants that biodegrade.

bioremediation Using bacteria and other microorganisms to treat chemical leaks or spills on soil or groundwater.

compost A mixture of decaying organic matter, such as food scraps and dead leaves, which is used to fertilize gardens.

consumer A user or buyer of a product.

farmer's market A market where farmers sell produce, meat, and other products directly to consumers.

fossil fuel Any material that is based on former life and can be burned, including oil, natural gas, and coal.

global warming An increase in the average temperature of Earth's atmosphere that causes changes in the climate.

greenhouse gas Any of the gases that absorb sunlight in the atmosphere and thus contribute to global warming.

greenwashing The practice of making a company or its products appear to be eco-friendly.

landfill A large hole in the ground in which a community's solid waste, or trash, is dumped. Landfills are carefully designed to prevent waste from mixing with soil and water in the ground and to reduce odors as the waste decomposes.

organic From a living organism; regarding food, something that is grown without chemical fertilizers or pesticides. Natural fertilizers and pesticides can be used on produce this is grown organically.

peat Dead plant tissues that have partially decomposed in water.

pesticide A chemical that is used to kill weeds or animal pests. A natural pesticide is made from a natural product that has undergone only a little processing.

polystyrene foam A plastic, often called foam, that is formed into small beads that are then made into a variety of throwaway containers.

solid waste Trash; materials that people use and then throw away.

sustainable Able to continue with minimal effects on the environment. A level of consumption that can be supplied by the environment without overtaxing it.

synthetic Man-made.

FOR MORE INFORMATION

Canadian Environmental Network (RCEN)
14 Manchester Avenue, Unit 2
OTTAWA ON
K1Y 1Y9
+1 (204) 898-6460
Website: http://www.rcen.ca
Facebook: @CanadianEnvironmentalNetwork
Twitter: @RCEN
Since 1977, the Canadian Environmental Network
    fosters networking among nonprofit, nongovernmen-
    tal environmental organizations across Canada and
    the world.

National Audubon Society
225 Varick Street, 7th Floor
New York, NY 10014
(212) 979-3196
Website: http://www.audubon.org
Facebook: @NationalAudobonSociety
Twitter and Instagram: @audobonsociety
The National Audubon Society is a conservation group
    that focuses on protecting birds and their habitats.

The Nature Conservancy
4245 North Fairfax Drive, Suite 100
Arlington, VA 22203-1606
(703) 841-5300
Website: http://www.nature.org
Facebook: @thenatureconservancy
Twitter and Instagram: @nature_org
YouTube: @natureconservancy

The Nature Conservancy is a preeminent conservation group that works around the world to protect ecologically important lands and waters.

Sierra Club
2101 Webster Street, Suite 1300
Oakland, CA 94612
(415) 977-5500
Website: http://www.sierraclub.org
Facebook, Twitter, and Instagram: @sierraclub
YouTube: @NationalSierraClub
The Sierra Club was founded by legendary conservationist John Muir in 1892. It has grown into one of the nation's largest and most influential environmental groups.

Worldwatch Institute
1776 Massachusetts Avenue NW
Washington, DC 20036
(202) 452-1999
Website: http://www.worldwatch.org
Facebook: @Worldwatch-Institute
Twitter: @Worldwatch
YouTube: @WorldwatchInst
This institute develops information and strategies about climate change, energy consumption, and population growth.

FOR FURTHER READING

Baker, David. *Earth Manual: A Step-By-Step Guide to How It Works*. Sparkford, England: Haynes Publishing, 2015.

Botkin, Daniel B., and Edward A. Keller. *Environmental Science: Earth as a Living Planet*. Hoboken, NJ: Wiley, 2014.

Cloos, Marla Esser. *Living Green Effortlessly: Simple Choices for a Better Home*. Washington, DC: NAHB, 2017.

Faires, Nicole. *The Ultimate Guide to Natural Farming and Sustainable Living: Permaculture for Beginners*. New York, NY: Skyhorse Publishing, 2016.

Grinspoon, David. *Earth in Human Hands: Shaping Our Planet's Future*. New York, NY: Grand Central, 2016.

Macdonald, Deanna. *Eco Living Japan: Sustainable Ideas for Living Green*. Tokyo, Japan: Tuttle Publishing, 2016.

Moss, Stephen. *Planet Earth II*. London, England: BBC Books, 2016.

Somerville, Madeleine. *All You Need Is Less: The Eco-Friendly Guide to Guilt-Free Green Living and Stress-Free Simplicity*. Berkeley, CA: Viva Editions, An Imprint of Cleis Press, Inc., 2014.

Strawbridge, Dick. *Self Sufficiency for the 21st Century*. London, England: DK Publishing, 2017.

BIBLIOGRAPHY

American Veterinary Medical Association. "Market Research Statistics." U.S. Pet Ownership & Demographics Sourcebook (2007 Edition). Retrieved September 10, 2008. http://www.avma.org/refer ence/marketstats/sourcebook.asp.

Becker, Jeff (Engineer, biocompatible and biobased products, Minnesota Technical Assistance Program, University of Minnesota), in discussion with the author, September 2008.

Clark, Duncan, and Richie Unterberger. *The Rough Guide to Shopping with a Conscience.* New York, NY: Penguin Group, 2007.

Earth911.com. Retrieved September 15, 2017. http://earth911.com.

EPA. Retrieved September 15, 2017. https://www.epa.gov.

Erwin, Caitlin. "List of Biodegradable, Every Day Products." LIVESTRONG.COM, June 13, 2017. http://www.livestrong.com/article/219138-list-of-biodegradable-every-day-products.

Erwin, Lewis, and L. Hall Healy. *Packaging and Solid Waste: Management Strategies.* New York, NY: American Management Association, 1990.

Grosvenor, Michael. *Sustainable Living for Dummies.* Milton, Australia: Wiley Publishing, 2007.

Horn, Greg. *Living Green: A Practical Guide to Simple Sustainability.* Topanga, CA: Freedom Press, 2006.

Little, Ken. *Socially Responsible Investing.* New York, NY: Penguin Group, 2008.

Loux, René. *Easy Green Living: The Ultimate Guide to Simple, Eco-Friendly Choices for You and Your*

Home. Emmaus, PA: Rodale, 2008.

National Geographic Society. "Great Pacific Garbage Patch." September 19, 2014. https://admin.national geographic.org/encyclopedia/great-pacific -garbage-patch.

Newton, David E. *Chemistry of the Environment.* New York, NY: Facts on File, 2007.

Pet Industry Market Size & Ownership Statistics. Retrieved September 15, 2017. http://www .americanpetproducts.org/press_industrytrends.asp.

Rogers, Elizabeth, and Thomas M. Kostigen. *The Green Book: The Everyday Guide to Saving the Planet One Simple Step at a Time.* New York, NY: Three Rivers Press, 2007.

Schiller, Ben. "Boy Genius Boyan Slat's Giant Ocean Cleanup Machine Is Real." *Fast Company,* June 30, 2017. https://www.fastcompany.com/40419899/boy -genius-boyan-slats-giant-ocean-cleanup-machine -is-real.

Uldrich, Jack. *Green Investing.* Avon, MA: Adams Media, 2008.

Wire Staff, The. "Cleaning a River in Two Months, and on a Budget." The Wire, September 14, 2017. https://thewire.in/176238/intach-assi-river -cleaning-varanasi.

INDEX

A

additives, 9

B

bacteria, 4, 44–45
bamboo, 11, 13, 16, 36, 40
bedroom, 36–37
bioplastics, 24–26, 47, 44–45
bioremediation, 44, 45, 46
bread, 4, 9, 26

C

cleaners, 22, 29–33, 35, 49
clothes, 4, 7, 11–12, 13, 14, 17, 19, 20, 24, 33, 35, 47
community-supported agriculture (CSA), 11
compost, 19, 22, 25–26
   home, 24, 26, 28, 32, 44, 52
   industrial, 24, 43–44, 52
   at restaurants, 16
computers, 4, 17, 50
consumer products, 6, 50
Consumer Product Safety Commission (CPSC), 32
cosmetics, 4
cotton, 7, 11, 12, 13

D

dog waste, 43

E

eco-investing, 46–48
EcoLogo, 50
eggs, 9
   cartons for, 20
Energy Star, 49–50
Environmental Protection Agency (EPA), 18, 19, 32

F

factory farms, 7–8
farmer's markets, 9, 10–11
fertilizers, 7, 8, 9, 26, 35, 39, 45
food waste, 16, 17, 18, 19, 24, 26, 28, 44
fossil fuels, 6, 10, 20, 24, 28, 31, 32, 33, 36, 40
fruits, 4, 7–8, 9, 11, 35, 40
   citrus, 33

G

garbage disposals, 28
global warming, 6, 24–25
grains, 7–8, 9, 10
gray water, 17, 27
Great Pacific Garbage Patch, 25
greenhouse gases, 6, 10, 14, 16, 17, 31–32
greenwashing, 48

ABOUT THE AUTHORS

Nicholas Faulkner is a writer living in New Jersey.

Judy Monroe Peterson has earned two master's degrees, including a master's in public health education, and is the author of numerous educational books for young people. She is a former health care, technical, and academic librarian and college faculty member; a biologist and research scientist; and a curriculum editor with more than twenty-five years of experience. She has taught courses at 3M, the University of Minnesota, and Lake Superior College. Currently, she is a writer and editor of K–12 and post–high school curriculum materials on a variety of subjects, including biology, life science, the environment, health, and life skills.

PHOTO CREDITS

Cover Ababsolutum/E+/Getty Images; pp. 4–5 (background) namtipStudio/Shutterstock.com; p. 5 Robert Daemmrich Photography Inc/Corbis Historical/Getty Images; pp. 7, 17, 29, 42 Evan Lome/Shutterstock.com; p. 8 © iStockphoto.com/monkeybusinessimages; p. 10 © iStockphoto.com/asiseeit; p. 12 danishkhan/E+/Getty Images; p. 14 SpeedKingz/Shutterstock.com; p. 18 vchal/Shutterstock.com; p. 21 Bloomberg/Getty Images; p. 23 ziggy1/iStock/Thinkstock; p. 27 Pridannikov/iStock/Thinkstock; pp. 30–31 holbox/Shutterstock.com; pp. 34–35 jml5571/E+/Getty Images; p. 37 Daxiao Productions/Shutterstock.com; pp. 38–39 fotokostic/iStock/Thinkstock; p. 43 Monika Wisniewska/Shutterstock.com; p. 47 Spencer Platt/Getty Images; pp. 50–51 Hero Images/Getty Images.

Design: Michael Moy; Photo Research: Karen Huang